PARKING

N

TAXI

A

I

H

G

I

J

K

L

THE LEGEND

1. HOLY MASS INTENTIONS
2. THE HALL OF OUR LADY MARY
3. THE HALL OF POPE PAUL II
4. THE INTRANCE TO THE
   STATIONS OF THE CROSS
5. THE BASILICA
6. THE CENACLE
7. THE ENTRANCE TO THE
   TREASURY AND CHAPEL
   SACRARIUM OF THE NATION
8. THE INFORMATION CENTER
9. THE ENTRANCE TO THE TOWER
10. FIRST AID STATION
11. THE ARSENAL
12. THE 600 ANNIVERSERY MUSEUM
13. THE ENTRANCE TO THE KNIGHT
    HALL AND MONASTERY
14. THE CHAPEL OF OUR LADY
15. THE RADIO „JASNA GÓRA"
16. TOILETS
17. THE GATE OF POPE
    JOHN PAUL II
18. JASNA GÓRA ROSARY FAMILY
    OFFICE
19. HOSPICIUM
20. THE MONUMENT OF FATHER
    AUGUSTYN KORDECKI
21. LEFT-LUGGUGE-OFFICE

I-XIV THE STATIONS OF THE CROSS

A GIFT SHOP „CLAROMONTANA"
B SOCALLED JOHN PAUL II
   PILGRIMS HOME
C MONUMENT OF JOHN PAUL II
   PARENTS
D CAFFETERIA
E TOILETS
F BAR
G HOTEL
H THE CHAPEL OF ST. JOSEPH
I HOUSE OF PILGRIMS *
J BOOKSTORE „CLAROMONTANA"
K POST OFFICE AND CANTOR
L BANK
M THE MONUMENT OF IMMACULATA

* CHILDREN OF MARY ASSOCIATION
* EDITOR'S OFFICE
  „STUDIA CLAROMONTANA"
* EDITOR'S OFFICE
  „JASNA GÓRA"
* DISPENSARY FOR JASNA GÓRA
* MARIAN LIBRARY
* SPOKESMAN OF JASNA GÓRA

JASNA GÓRA

THE SANCTUARY OF THE MOTHER OF GOD

JAN PACH   WŁODZIMIERZ ROBAK   JERZY TOMZIŃSKI

JASNA GÓRA

THE SANCTUARY
OF THE MOTHER OF GOD

WYDAWNICTWO ZAKONU PAULINÓW

- 69 -

Jasna Góra - Częstochowa

1999

Photography:
Krzysztof Świertok
The Archiv of Jasna Góra

Graphics:
Grzegorz Górnikiewicz

Chief Editor:
Elżbieta Cichoń - Dziąba

Graphic Elaboration:
Jerzy Mac
Dariusz Kryśkow

Front Cover:
Jerzy Mac

ISBN 83-903854-7-3
Pauline Order Publication
PAULINIANUM
Jasna Góra
Częstochowa, Poland 1999

ISBN 83-908114-3-X
Publisher „DAWIT"
Katowice, Poland 1999

Published by „DAWIT"
ul. Franciszkańska 29-31;   40-708 Katowice, Poland
tel. (0-32) 25-26-002 w. 42; (0-601) 41 62 60; (0-601) 41 62 67

INDEX

1. AN HISTORICAL OUTLINE

On the limehills extending from Kraków to Wielun ("land of the eagle's nest") on the River Warta, rises the city of Częstochowa, the capital of the province of the same name. It is believed that the name of the city derives from its founder, a Slav called Czestoch. In 13th century documents, it is mentioned as a village of horsemen called Czenstochowa and at the end of the 14th century, it received its charter.

In the western part of the city, known as "old Częstochowa" in the 14th century, a 293-metre high hill was handed over to the Pauline Monks from Hungary in 1382. A sanctuary and monastery were built on the site, surrounded by a wall and garden and it bore the name Jasna Góra (Bright Hill). The name was taken from that of their Mother House at Buda, St. Lawrence in Claro Monte Budensi.

The Pauline Monks belonged to the Order of St. Paul the First Hermit, founded at the beginning of the 13th century in Hungary in the wake of the great Hermit movement that swept Europe between the 12th

and 13th centuries. The Order's founder, the Blessed Eusebius, Canon of Esztergom, founded the first community of Paulines by uniting all the hermits who lived in the forests of Hungary and Croatia. They modelled their monastic life on St. Augustine and they chose St. Paul of Thebes, the First Hermit, as their Patriarch.

Born in Thebes probably in the year 230, Paul fled into the surrounding desert when he was only 16 years old during the persecutions of Decian. According to the tradition passed down from St. Jerome, he lived in the desert for 90 years on a diet of bread, brought to him by a raven. St. Jerome tells us that at the end of his life, St Anthony, abbot had sought him out and, according to legend, buried Paul's body in a grave dug by two lions. This is why the symbol of the Order of the Pauline Monks shows a palm tree, two lions and a raven with bread in its beak. It was Prince Ladislaus of Opole, the plenipotentiary of King Louis of Hungary for Polish territory between 1367 and 1372 who summoned the Pauline Monks to Poland. They arrived in Częstochowa in 1382 and were given a small church where they kept the Miraculous Painting of Our Lady which the Prince had brought from the city of Bełz in Ukraine.

There are two versions of the history of the Jasna Góra painting. There is a traditional version steeped in legend and an historical one, reconstructed by art critics whose attention was drawn to this extraordinary image and its origins.

According to the traditional version, the painting was executed by St. Luke the Evangelist on a table top from the house of the Holy Family. St. Luke was said to have painted two images of Mary, one of which found its way to Italy and was kept in Bologna where it is still venerated. The other was said to have been removed from Jerusalem and brought to Constantinople by the Emperor Constantine and placed in a church Six centuries later, the Russian

The Coat of Arms of the Pauline Order

Prince Lev obtained the painting from the emperor of the time in acknowledgement of his military achievements. During the wars in Ruś, Prince Ladislaus of Opole found the painting in the castle at Bełz and discovered it was being venerated as if it were miraculous. After the victory over the Tatars, he brought the painting to Częstochowa, entrusting it to the Pauline Monks for safekeeping. This information is contained in a manuscript - one of the oldest - entitled "Translatio Tabulae", a copy of which, dated 1474, is conserved in the Jasna Góra archives.

According to art critics, the Jasna Góra painting was originally a Byzantine icon (of the Hodigitria type), dating between the sixth and ninth centuries.

The growing fame of the miraculous image of the Mother of God meant that in a short time, the monastery became the site of constant pilgrimages and the costodian of numerous, priceless votive offerings. But, unfortunately, such valuable gifts led to greed. On Easter Day April 14, 1430, a gang of robbers from Bohemia, Moravia and Silesia attacked the monastery.

They burst into the Chapel of the Mother of God and grabbed the image from the altar. They then stole all the painting's valuable gift offerings and disfigured it slashing it with their swords.

They threw the painting to the ground and it broke in three places, according to the account of Piotr Risinus in the 1523 volume "Historia Pulchra".

Prince Ladislaus of Opole presents the Holy Icon to the Pauline Order

The painting was restored at Kraków, at the court of King Ladislaus Jagiełło. Restorers tried repeatedly to spread colour on the panel but the shades kept vanishing. Today, it is known that in the Middle Ages, restorers had difficulty working on an ancient icon because of the application of tempera colours on an image obtained with shades diluted with fused wax. Because the restoration operation was a total failure, the restorers scraped away the ancient image and painted a completely new one over the miraculous panel. They marked the signs of the robbers' outrage on the face of the image with a pen, in memory of the barbarism. After the painting's profanation and restoration, the sancuary's fame grew even more. There were more and more pilgrimages to the site and soon the original gothic church proved too small to cater for the vast numbers of faithful. So in the 1460s, building was begun beside the Chapel to Our Lady on a new gothic church with three wide aisles.

In 1466, the monastery was attacked again, by the army of the Bohemian King. These raids and the need for a protective bulwark near the border with Silesia convinced King Ladislaus IV to erect a wall round the monastery. Work was begun in 1638 transforming the Jasna Góra sanctuary into a Marian Fortress - Fortalitium Marianum. But it would not be long before the sancturary would be put to the test again. At about 1655, a plan for attacking Poland was devised and on July 21 that year, the Swedish Army marched on the country. Warsaw, Poznań and Kraków soon fell. The Polish nobility, divided by internecine disputes, refused to fight and the whole country fell under Swedish dominion. On November 18, 1655, General Müller's army of 3,000 men reached Jasna Góra demanding the sanctuary's immediate surrender. Nevertheless, Jasna Góra's Prior, Augustine Kordecki decided to defend the holy site. He could count on 170 soldiers, 20 noblemen and 70 monks, too few to stand up to the 3,000 Swedish invaders.

When the monks refused to surrender, the Swedish army opened their attack which was to last 40 days but which would end in victory for Mary's army. The victory secured by the tiny Jasna Góra fortress, which General Müller scathingly called the "henhouse", proved to be of great

Profanation of the Holy Icon in 1430.
Painting from the 17th century
in the Knights' Hall

religious and political importance. The attack on Jasna Góra was considered a violation of religious sentiments and political importance. The attack on Jasna Góra was considered a violation of religious sentiments and the victorious result was ascribed not to the military skill of the soldiers nor to the solidity of the fortress but to protection by the Mother of God herself, guardian of the site. After the Jasna Góra victory, the whole country rose up against the Swedish invaders.

On April 1, 1656, in the cathedral of Lvov, King John Casimirus solemnly pronounced his vow to consecrate the country to the protection of the Mother of God and proclaimed Her the Patron and Queen of the lands in his kingdom. The nation's destiny was entrusted to the Most Blessed Virgin from that moment. Jasna Góra became a symbol of religious and political liberty for the Polish people. But the fortifications of the Marian bulwark would have to stave off more attacks, in 1656, 1702, 1704 and 1705.

From 1711, Poland lived in relative peace. It was the time to crown the Effigy to Our Lady. The faithful had been requesting this for a long time and a crown had been placed on the image as far back as the sanctuary's foundation according to lithographs of the 16th century.

On the occasion of the Apostolic Nuncio, Benedetto Odescalchi, the Pauline monks made enquiries about organising the crowning of the image. They had drawn favourable replies and formally presented their request to the Vatican Chapter. In 1716, Pope Clement XI signed the Act of Incoronation and it took place on September 8, 1717 in presence of about 200,000 faithful.

The siege of Jasna Gora in 1655.
A painting depicting this event can be found
in the Arsenal

Halfway through the 18th century, the precarious political system, the growing power and dominion of the Polish aristocracy and misguided foreign policy led to the decline of the republic. Neighbouring states - Russia and

Knights armor (15th century)

Prussia - took advantage and on the pretext of protecting Poland, the army of the Russian Empress Catherine II marched in. On January 29, 1768, a Confederation of Polish aristocrats was formed to combat King Stanley Poniatowski who fostered Russia's interests. Casimir Pułaski, one of the Confederation's leaders, occupied the Jasna Góra fortress and for three years, he

defended it against Russian attacks. When the Confederation disbanded in September 1772, King Stanley Poniatowski ordered that the fortress be handed over to the Russians. It was the first time an enemy army ever penetrated the walls of Jasna Góra. Poland was partitioned a short time afterwards. In 1795, Poland was partitioned for a third time by three invaders - the Austrians, the Prussians and the Russians - and for over 120 years Poland was cancelled from the map of Europe.

During this unhappy period, Jasna Góra was a point of reference for the divided nation. It made Poles aware that they were sons of one land and inspired hope for liberty in their hearts. The image of Our Lady thus became a pledge for a free Poland.

At the time of Napoleon I when Warsaw was a principality Jasna Góra became a military fortress for the last time. It was called to defend the liberty of the Polish people who resisted a series of attacks by enemy armies between 1806 and 1813.

When Napoleon fell, the Russian army again occupied the fortress of Jasna Góra and the Tsar Alesander I ordered that its walls be demolished. It was only in 1843 by order of Tsar Nicholas I that the walls were rebuilt, although to different plans.

By issuing such an order the Tsar hoped that he would

appear tolerant and benevolent towards the Church in the eyes of all Europe. But all three invaders feared Jasna Góra because of its special role as defender of the faith and homeland. They therefore forbade Polish people to make pilgrimages to Częstochowa and called Our Lady

ordered that the printing house, the pharmacy and all the religious offices of Jasna Góra be closed. He stripped the monastery of its land and set limits on the number of monks who could live there. Even the right to retreat was repressed and the Czar's men harassed the

The Bar Confederates defend Jasna Gora in 1771 (1982)

of Jasna Góra "the biggest revolutionary of them all".

In such a climate, insurrection came soon, in Janurary 1863, with the aim of liberating Poland. The rebels carred banners bearing the image of Our Lady of Jasna Góra but the insurrection was repressed and the whole nation later suffered the consequences. Many Pauline monks were also accused of collaborating with the rebels and deported to Siberia. In 1864, Tsar Alexander II

monks continually. On the night of September 22, 1909, the pearl vestment and two gold crowns, which were papal gifts, were stolen from the Miraculous Painting. When Pope Pius X heard about the theft he offered two new crowns to the Jasna Góra painting. The new incoronation took place on May 22, 1910 and although the partition of Poland was again under way, it was celebrated amid the same splendour as the 1717 ceremony.

Jasna Góra emerged unscathed from World War I and from then until World War II, it would again be the focal point of important historical events. On July

Warsaw, thousands of Poles travelled to Jasna Góra to their Queen to beg her for victory, which duly came on August 15, the Feast of the Assumption. This victory, called the "miracle of the Vistula" was attributed to Our Lady's intercession. In 1932, the 550th anniversary of the transfer of the Effigy of Mary from Bełz to Jasna Góra was celebrated. That year 750,000 pilgrims travelled to the sancturary. In May 1936, 20,000 Polish students consecrated their lives to Mary vowing to build with Her new Poland. In August the same year, the first plenary synod of the Polish Episcopate met at Jasna Góra. With the start of World War II, the whole country was put to a bitter test and Jasna Góra was no exception.

The Image of Our Blessed Lady adorned with a diamond robe and crown

27, 1920 with the Russian Bolshevik scourge close at hand, the Polish Episcopate met at Jasna Góra and again proclaimed Mary, Queen of Poland. When the Red Army reached

Part of the monastery was invaded by Nazi troops who remained there until January 16, 1945. Although organised pilgrimages were prohibited, those who managed to reach the sancturary were comforted by messages of hope from the pulpit. At Jasna Góra, partisans, prisoners and Jews found succour.

On January 16, 1945 while monks were secretly holding lessons for young people, the sanctuary was suddenly attacked by the Red Army. The Germans who had taken possession of the sanctuary panicked and fled. They had had no time to spirit its treasures away or destroy the monastery.

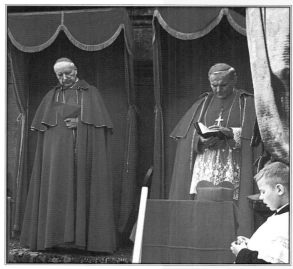

Cardinal Stefan Wyszynski, Primate of Poland and Cardinal Karol Wojtyla at Jasna Gora for the Millenium celebrations on May, 3rd 1966

After the War, Jasna Góra was once more the nation's spiritual capital. In September 1946 before half a million faithful, the then Polish Primate August Hlond consecrated Poland to Mary's Immaculate Heart.

In 1948, when Communist ideology threatened, the Primate's message on his death-bed would prove to be prophetic. "Victory when it comes, will be a victory of the Most Blessed Mother", was the message which would be the inheriance of the new Primate, Stefan Wyszyński.

Jailed by Communists in a Stalinist prison, Cardinal Wyszyński would draw inspiration from the gesture of King John Casimirus and composed a prayer to the Virgin in which he expressed his gratitude for all the grace received. He incorpora-

ted a prayer for a free Poland and an immaculate life in thanks for liberty. On August 26, 1956 the 300th anniversary of King John Casimir's vow, the cardinal's prayer was read publicly for the first time, at Jasna Góra before a million faithful. Cardinal Wyszyński, who was in jail at that time, was finally released on October 26.

In 1957, Pope Pius XII blessed a copy of the Jasna Góra effigy that was to be taken from parish to parish throughout the nation. It travelled the country for 25 years and was to bring about numerous conversions. On May 3, 1966, the occasion of the millenium of Poland's conversion to Christianity, the whole Polish Episcopate ratified the Act of the Consecration of Poland "In Service to Mary, Mother of the Church, for the Liberty of the Church of Christ". Pope Paul VI expressed his desire to visit Jasna Góra on the occasion of this Act to honour the sanctuary with the gift of a golden rose. But the Communist regime would not allow it.

One June 4, 1979, the first Polish Pope, John Paul II, visited and where I used to kneel on the bare ground like you often do for hours and hours..." During his three-day visit, the Pope encountered three and a half million faithful. John Paul II declared the faith of the Universal Church, of his homeland, of all mankind and of himself in the Virgin and proclaimed

Pope John Paul II at Jasna Gora (1991)

Jasna Góra and began his pilgrimage with these words: "Mary's will is being fulfilled. Here I am... I have come and I recall an old song of the Bar confederates: "We ares servants of Christ, servants of Mary..." The servant called from this land, summoned from the foot of Jasna Góra where I used to stop like you do "Mother, I am yours and all that I have is yours". He made on offering of a golden rose and set it on the altar of the Mother of God.

The sanctuary celebrated its 600th anniversary in 1982 although on December 13, 1981, relations between the government and the population worsened after the

Northside view of Jasna Gora

Communists declared a state of narial law. This meant the Holy Father would not be present at the Jubilee Year and he would not return until June the next year. It was a visit that brought hope and comfort to the Polish people in their struggle for freedom. Jasna Góra would host the Pope a third time, in 1987 on the occasion of the Polish Eucharistic Congress.

The Holy Father often prayed that the precarious politico-economic situation in Poland would not dampen the people's hopes for a better future. The Polish people's faith in the intercession of the Virgin of Jasna Góra has continued to find expression in the increasing number of pilgrims to the sanctuary. In the past few years, over four million pil-

Pilgrims on their way to Jasna Gora.

FORTALITIUM MARIANUM THE FORTRESS SANCTURARY OF JASNA GÓRA

1. *The Lubomirski Gate*
2. *The Queen of Poland Gate*
3. *The Our Lady of Sorrows Gate*
4. *The Jagiellonian Gate*
5. *The Bells*
6. *The Marian Room*
7. *The Basilica*
8. *The Chapel of St. Paul the First Hermit*
9. *The Chapel of the Most Sacred Heart of Jesus*
10. *The Chapel of the Virgin*
11. *The Horsemen's Hall*
12. *The Sacristy*
13. *The Cenaculum*
14. *The Monastery*

15. *The Royal Rooms*
16. *The Chapel of National Memory*
17. *The 600-Year Museum*
18. *The Arsenal*
19. *The John Paul II door*
20. *The Treasure*
21. *The St. Barbara Bastion*
22. *The St. Rocco Bastion*
23. *The Holy Trinity Bastion*
24. *The St. James Bastion*
25. *The monument to Fr. Kordecki*

I-XIV The Stations of the Cross

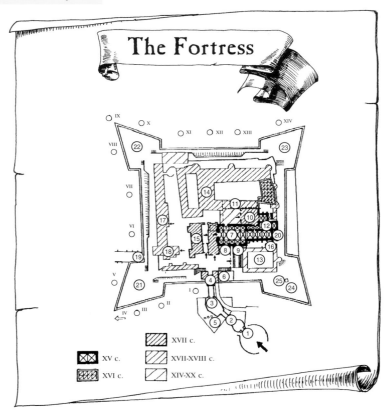

grims have travelled to Jasna Góra, about 350,000 of them on foot.

The last decade bears witness to the Polish people's deepening devotion for Jasna Góra. The failure and fall of Communism called the "new miracle of the Vistula", were planned in prayer before the face of Our Lady. For the faithful who strive to put Mary's testament into practice, "Whatsoever he saith unto you, do it" (John 2:5), Mary is the protagonist of Poland's revolution of love. Thanks to her presence and her maternal intercession, Christ lives in history.

The Jasna Góra sancturary, situated on a plain, its belltower dominating the city of Częstochowa, is visible from tens of kilometers away. It occupies an area of five hectares. A park surrounds the

West side view of Jasna Gora

monastery on three sides while the fourth opens onto a large square for crowds of pilgrims at major liturgical functions. A public park extends from the square down the valley to the city forming a natural barrier to preserve the spiritual, prayerful atmosphere of the sanctuary. The Jasna Góra complex was built over five centuries but is architecturally compact.

The walls of the fortress ensure the safekeeping of the treasures of faith and Polish culture conserved in the Jasna Góra monastery.

Four doors, built between the 17th and 19th centuries, provide access to the monastery proper. The central part of the

Lubomirski`s Gate

The Cenaculum

buildings is the oldest and others were built around it down the centuries in a type of circle. The Chapel of the Virgin (between the 17th and 20th centuries), the Basilica (between the 15th and 17th centuries) and the Cenacle (20th century) from the heart of the monastery.

Beside the holy site are the so-called King's Chambers (17th century), the royal apartament for monarchs on pilgrimages to the sanctuary.

The monastery comprises two square buildings (15th and 17th century) interconnected by a 17th century wing, which hosts priests or

pilgrimages today, and the old arsenal (17th century).

Beyond the fortress' walls, are the splendid and modern Stations of the Cross.

Reconciliation booths

The monastery courtyard

2. THE BELLTOWER

Rising above the architectural complex of Jasna Góra is the splendid belltower (Which is 106 meters and 30 cm's tall).

This belltower, damaged several times in fires, was reconstructed in 1906. The lower part dates to 1714 and is in the baroque style. Externally, at the height of the second floor, there are four clocks on each of the tower's sides. All the clocks are worked by a single mechanism of 36 bells which ring Marian melodies every 15 minutes. Inside on the third level, there are four statues, one in each corner: St. Paul the Hermit, St. Florian, St. Casimir and the Saint and Queen, Hedvig.

On the fifth level 516 steps up, more statues have been erected representing the fathers of the Church. St. Leo the Great, St. Gregory, St. Augustine and St. Ambrose.

A raven with bread in its beak (the symbol of the Pauline Order) is on top of the tower's spire with a monogram of the Blessed Virgin Mary. The monogram is topped by a cross which is illuminated at night, symbolising the light that emanates from this holy place.

Jasna Gora Monastery 3rd. May Park

The Tower

3. THE ICON OF THE VIRGIN

Jasna Góra's most valuable treasure is the miraculous painting of Our Lady. Because of this painting, Jasna Góra became Poland's most famous sanctuary among the numerous sites to Marian devotion throughout the country. But it is not just the tradition, which considers Luke the Apostle as the artist, or the influence of monarchs to whom Jasna Góra has always been dear that made this place famous above all others. It is the Miraculous pre

The Holy Icon of Our Blessed Mother of Jasna Gora

ence of the image which has always attracted pilgrims not only from all over Poland but from all over the world, as the numerous votive offerings show.

The painting of Our Lady is the very core of Jasna Góra drawing crowds of pilgrims to it. This sanctury was not built after a Marian apparition as is usually the case for major holy sites. Without the painting, Jasna Góra would be nothing but a building complex, a museum of artworks which are undoubtedly precious and beautiful but devoid of any vitality. The painting is the mytery, the fulchrum, the atmosphere of the Jasna Góra sancturary.

It was painted on a wood panel measuring 122.2 x 82.2 x 3.5 cms. and features a bust of the Virgin with Jesus in her arms. Mary's face dominates the painting and observers find themselves immersed in her eyes. They look at Mary, who looks back at them.

The face of the Child is also turned towards the pilgrim but his eyes are looking elsewhere. The two faces have a serious and thoughtful expression adding to the emotional tone of the painting. Our Lady's right cheek is marked by two parallel slashes and a third horizontal cut. The neck of the image is marred with six scratches, two more visible than others. Jesus, dressed in a scarlet tunic is supported by His Mother's left arm. He is holding a book in His left hand, his right hand is raised in a magisterial gesture, of sovereignty

and benediction. The hand of the Virgin rests on Her breast, as if she were indicating the Child. The Virgin's robe and mantle are decorated with lilies, the symbol of the Hungarian royal family. A six-pointed star is featured on Mary's brow. An important element are the auras around the Virgin and Child since their luminous quality contrasts with the dark facial tones.

The painting of the Virgin belongs to the group of Hodigitria icons "she who indicates and guides along the road").

The Jasna Góra icon represents the Biblical message and invites prayer and reflection.

4. THE CHAPEL OF THE VIRGIN

The Virgin's many miracles in the holy place are at the origin of the whole Jasna Góra complex and the painting with the image of Her is the sanctuary's core. In 1382, the Pauline monks received the gift of a small church from Prince Ladislaus of Opole. It was built in wood and the prince also gave the monks an effigy of the Blessed Virgin. The first pilgrimages began soon afterwards and the church soon proved to be too small to host the numbers of faithful. Thus, in the early 15th century in the reign of Ladislaus Jagiełło, a gothic chapel was built. This original gothic part of the chapel (now the presbytery) ends at the point where an enormous iron grating extends from the floor to the ceiling, and has a later date (1600). Between 1642 and 1644, a church with three aisles was bult onto the gothic chapel, constructed in the typically Polish style known as "Lublin Baroque", a mixture of Mannerism and the Baroque. The construction is one of the most important of the Counter-Reformation.

The sacred icon was later set on an altar of ebony and silver, a votive offering of the Grand Chancellor George Ossoliński in 1650, and it is still in the same place today. The silver panel protecting the icon is dated 1673.

The chapel has five altars but one in particular attracts atten-tion because of its considerable artis-tic merit. It has a cross of the yea 1400, of the Wit Stwosz school.

The walls of the chapel ar covered with votive offerings i thanks for the grace and miracle received after intercession by th Mother of God.

The third section of th chapel was built recently (1929). It pilars and walls are decorated wit votive plaques commemoratin Polish soldiers who fought in th World Wars or who were martyre under Communism.

A left wall niche contain the cinerary urn of Fr. Augustin Kordecki, Jasna Góra's defende against the Swedes

THE CHAPEL OF THE VIRGIN OF JASNA GÓRA

1. *The Altar of the Icon*
2. *The presbytery grille*
3. *The Altar of the Pieta*
4. *The Altar of the Presentation to the Temple of the Virgin*
5. *The Altar of the Visitation*
6. *The Altar of the Annunciation*
7. *The Altar of the Nativity of Mary*
8. *The Ambo*
9. *The Altar of the Crucifix*
10. *Stained glass windows*
11. *The Sacristy*

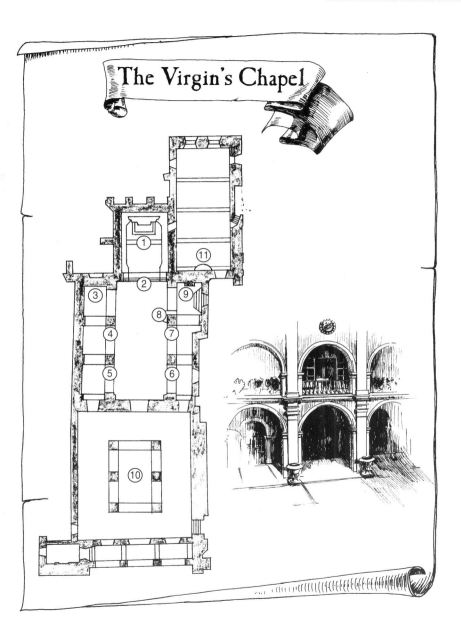

The Virgin's Chapel

Entrance to the Chapel of Our Lady

Jasna Gora`s Orchestra

The miraculous painting covered by the silver screen from 1673

The Chapel of The Mother of God – The Iron grating gates diriding the presbytery from the chapel (1644)

The golden rose – a gift from Pope John Paul II in 1979

The golden heart – a gift from Pope John Paul II after the attempt on his life at St. Peter's Square

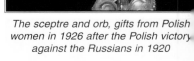

The sceptre and orb, gifts from Polish women in 1926 after the Polish victory against the Russians in 1920

New Organ (1990) in the Chapel of Our Lady

(Side) Altar in the Chapel of the Virgin with a 16th century Pieta

The Chapel of the Virgin Mary. The right hand altar (18th century) with the Crucifix (15th century)

The interior of the Chapel

Right wall adorned with votive offerings

5. THE BASILICA

The Church of the Holy Cross and Nativity of Mary beside the Chapel of the Virgin received the title and privileges of a Minor Basilica in 1906. It is 46 meters long, 21 meters wide and 29 meters high. The basilica's construction was begun in the early 15th century.

The interior of the Basilica

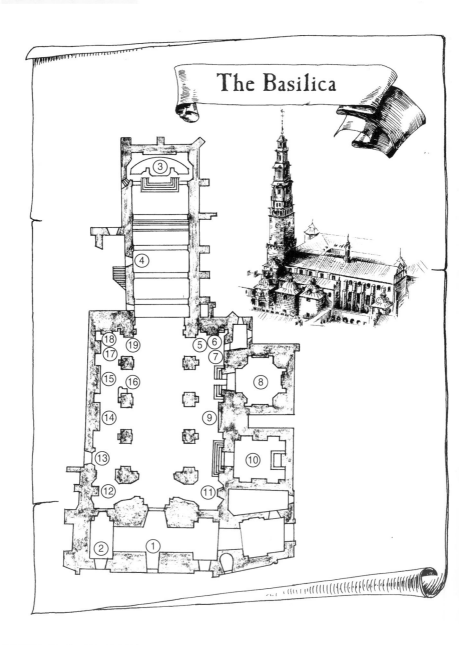

The Basilica

THE BASILICA OF THE HOLY CROSS AND THE NATIVITY OF MARY

1. The narthex
2. The Chapel of St. Anthony of Padua
3. The main altar
4. The sacristy entrance
5. The Altar of St. Anne
6. The Altar of St. Joseph
7. A. group sculpture featuring St. Francis Saverio
8. Above: The Chapel of the Most Sacred Heart of Jesus (the Jabłonowski family)
9. The Altar of the Three Magi
10. The Chapel of St. Paul the First Hermit (the Denhoff family)
11. The Altar of St. Casimir
12. The Altar of St. Maximilian Kolbe
13. Portal featuring St. Anthony Abbot and St. Paul the First Hermit
14. The Altar of the Nativity of Jesus
15. The Altar of St. Augustine
16. The Ambo
17. A statue of St. Stanisław, Bishop
18. The altar of St. John Nepomuceno
19. The Altar of Our Lady of the Rosary

The Basilica. The great organ of 1956

The Main Altar. The Assumption of Our Blessed Virgin Mary into heaven

In a fire in 1690 , the gothic vault collapsed and its rich internal decoration was burned. Today, the basilica which was rebuilt between 1692 and 1695 and restored in 1706 and 1728, has three aisles and is a fine example of Baroque art. The multi-coloured vaults of the presbytery and the main aisle are the work of Karl Dankwart (1695) and feature respectively the history of the Holy Cross and the miracles attributed to the mediation of the Virgin of Jasna Góra.

The ancient choirstalls are splendid with a 105-tone organ (about 8,000 pipes) and four registers. It is dated 1956 but is encased in an 18th century structure above the

Basilica. Ambo

basilica's entrance.

Along the basilica's right-hand aisle is a chapel made entirely of black marble dedicated to St. Paul the First Hermit. Towards the presbytery, there is a second chapel which also has special architectural features. It is divided in two sections, one over the other and dedicated to the Sacred Heart of Jesus and the Holy Relics.

A chapel to St. Anthony of Padua is to be found in the basilica's vestibule. It dates to the 17th century.

The main altar, designed by Giacomo Antonio Buzzini, was built between 1725 and 1728 and represents the Assumption. The grandeur of its marble makes it a fine example of Italian Baroque sculpture.

The Basilica, Main Altar (1725–1734)

*The portals of the Chapel of the Most Sacred Heart of Jesus,
below of the Holy Relies (1751)*

The Chapel of St. Paul the First Hermit (1674)

6. THE SACRISTY

Bult in 1651, the Sacristy is located between the Basilica and the Chapel of the Virgin. It is 19 meters long and ten meters wide.

The multi-coloured vault, the work of Karl Dankwart, was completed in 1693. Wall paintings of the 17th century depict the lives of the hermits and of the first anchorites of the Christian tradition.

The sacristy closets date to the second half of the 17th century. In front of the entrance, there is the altar of St. Wenceslaus with a painting of the crucified Christ.

A Dębnik marble faunt stands near the entrance and is dated 1740.

The Sacristy (1651)

7. THE TREASURY

Between 1649 and 1653, a room was built above the sacristy to safeguard the Jasna Góra treasure. At the beginning of this century, the room was restored by the architect Szyszko Bogusz. The treasure comprises many votive offerings of inestimable value such as ostensors, chalices and precious gems. Commemorative and devotional objects are also featured and express the pilgrims' innermost feelings: suffering, joy, gratitude. Also to be found are the votive offerings of the survivors of the concentration camps and apart from these objects' material value, they express the heartfelt gratitude of the donors. For this reason, the treasure is more a testimony of faith by entire generations, who offered gifts to their Mother and Queen in the course of six centuries. The oldest of these gifts date from the 14th century. The most significant and precious are of the 17th and early 18th centuries. Despite the wars and Poland's 100-year-long partition, most of the votive offerings have survived. In the 17th century the Pauline Monks started registering them and this custom survives today.

So, from the 17th century, the treasure constituted a type of artistc museum for the safekeeping of works of art in gold, precious textiles, armeries and jewels. Of particular beauty are the gifts of King Michael Korybut Wiśniowiecki and the Archduchess Eleanor of Austria on the occasion of their wedding in Jasna Góra in 1670.

Others include an ostensor of 1510, the gift of King Sigmund I, an ostensor belonging to Fr. Kordecki of 1672; Meissen porcelaine, the gift of King Augustus III of Saxony; a Holy Cross reliquary of 1721; a 15th century cassock, gift of the King of Hungary; the liturgical vestments of Canon Michael Krassowski, of 1725. Some gifts of recent popes are also preserved here: an ostensor and a chalice of the Second Vatican Council offered by Pope John XXIII and a chalice of Pope Paul VI.

The Treasury

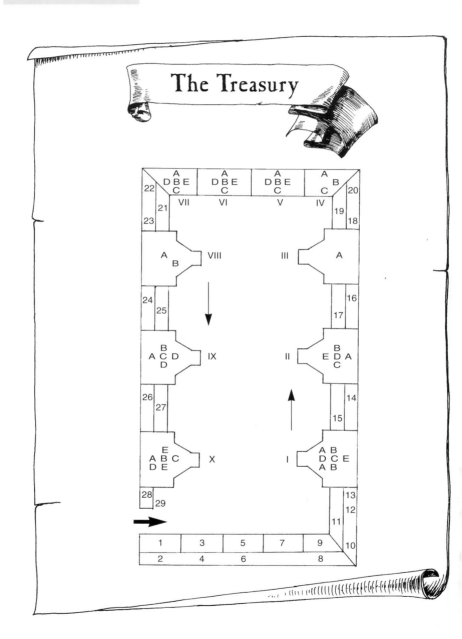

THE TREASURY

I. Show-Case

A. *Reliquaries and candelabra in silver (XVII-XVIII centuries)*
B. *Liturgical ornaments, a gift of King Michael Korybut Wiśniowiecki in 1870, a Sicilian work (XVII century)*
C. *Ostensory and candelabra, gift of the Austrian Imperial family, a Hapsburg work (XVI century)*
D. *Gilded silver chalice, a gift of Francis Lubomirski, a Viennese work (1743)*
E. *A votive altar, a gift of Prince Constantine Sobieski in 1709, a Hapsburg work (1624)*

II. Show-Case

A. *Russian icons (XVI-XVIII centuries)*
B. *Ivory miniatures: altar, coffer and chapel, the work and gift of Tadeus Kościuszko (XIX century); an amber statuette of the Virgin, from Gdańsk, the gift of Abbot David Konarski (XVI century)*
C. *Mother-of-pearl shell, the gift of Ludwig Pociej (XVII century); gilded silver chalice, the gift of King John III Sobieski, a Hapsburg work (XVII century)*
D. *Gilded bronze clock, the gift of King John III Sobieski, a Hapsburg work (XVII century)*
E. *Bronze and alabaster clocks (XIX century)*

III. Show-Case

A. *Meissen porcelain, the gift of King August III of Saxony in 1744*

IV. Show-Case

A. *A votive painting; Reliquary of the Holy Cross in crystal, a Viennese work (1703); vases and candelabra in crystal (XVI-XVII centuries), the gift of Queen Mary Josephine in 1744*
B. *Cross in crystal, the gift of King Stephen Batory, a Polish work (XVI century)*
C. *Rosary in crystal, the gift of Queen Eleanor*

V. Show-Case

A. *Ostensorium in silver, the gift of King Siegmund I, a Cracow work (1542)*
B. *The sceptre of King Siegmund August (XVI century)*
C. *Silver tray, the gift of King John III Sobieski, a Hapsburg work (XVII century)*
D. *Silver candelabra (XVI-XVIII centuries)*

VI. Show-Case

A. *Silver cross, the gift of King Siegmund I, originally a Nurimberg work (1510)*
B. *The Rosary of Queen Bona Sforza (XVI century)*
C. *Silver tray, the gift of King John III Sobieski, a Hapsburg work (XVII century)*
D. *Reliquary in silver, the gift of Bishop Otto Schenking (1606)*
E. *The cross of St. Carlo Borromeo, an Italian work (XV century)*

VII. Show-Case

A. *A reproduction of the Icon (XVIII century)*
B. *Reliquary, the gift of Bishop Hohn Thurzon (1511)*

C. *The Madonna and Child, the gift of the German Episcopate (1980)*
D. *"The Chalice of Life", the gift of Polish women (1982)*
E. *Chalice, the gift of the French Episcopate (1982)*

VIII. Show-Case

A. *Meissen porcelain, the gift of King August III of Saxony in 1744*
B. *Chinese porcelain (XX century)*

IX. Show-Case

A. *Monstrance in gold, the gift of Polish Americans (1934)*
B. *Chalice, the gift of Bishop James Malone (1985)*
C. *Silver chalice (XVII century)*
D. *Silver candelabra (XVI century); reliquaries in silver (XVII century)*

X. Show-Case

A. *Gilded silver and ivory ostensory, the gift of Pope John XXIII*
B. *Chalices, the gifts of Pope John Paul II and Pope Paul VI*
C. *Crystal chalice, the gift of the Austrian Episcopate (1983)*
D. *The First Communion veil of St. Theresa*
E. *The gift of concentration camp survivors*

1. *Amber gems (XIX-XX centuries)*
2. *A gothic chasuble, the gift of Hungarian Paulites (XV century)*
3. *Gems in mother-of-pearl and ivory (XIX-XX centuries)*
4. *Christ, an oil painting on wood (XVII century)*
5. *Jewellry (XVI-XVIII centuries)*
6. *Madonna and Child, a painting by John Matejko (XIX century)*

7. *Jewellry (XVI-XVIII centuries)*
8. *A chasuble, the gift of Queen Edwige (end-XV centruy)*
9. *Jewellry (XVIII-XX centuries)*
10. *Statue of Our Lady of Pilar, the gift of the Archibishop of Saragozza (1965)*
11. *Gems in coral and turquoise (XIX-XX centuries)*
12. *Altar in ebony and silver, the gift of Prince Constantine Sobieski, a Hapsburg work (1624)*
13. *The Virgin defends Jasna Góra from Swedish attacks (1655), an oil painting by John Matejko (XIX century)*
14. *Chasubles, the gifts of Princess Anna Orzelska, Queen Cecilia Renata, King Siegmund III Waza, Queen Anna Caterina, Prince Charles Ferdinand Waza (XVII-XVIII centuries)*
15. *Vatican coins and medals (XVI-XX centuries)*
16. *LIturgical vestments, the gift of Michale Krassowski (1720)*
17. *Watches and gold jewellery (XVIII-XX centuries)*
18. *Vestments of the Image (1982)*
19. *Jewellry (XVII-XX centuries)*
20. *Chasubles, the gitfs of Cardinal Vidoni, of Popielowa Koszbogowa, of the Arch-Priest of the Marian Church of Cracow (XVII-XVIII centuries)*
21. *Gold filigree (XVIII-XX centuries)*
22. *Rosaries (XVI-XX centuries)*
23. *Chasubles, the gifts of Duninówna Unichowska, Queen Eleanor, Casimir Brzostowski (XVII-XVIII centuries)*
24. *Liturgical vestments (XIX century)*
25. *Jewellry (XIX-XX centuries)*
26. *Chasubles, the gifts of Queen Bona Sforza, Queen Constance, Prince John Sobieski, Anna Denhoff, Queen Mary Josephine (XVI-XVII centuries)*
27. *Jewellry (XIX-XX centuries)*
28. *Cope, the gift of Princess Anna Orzelska (1727)*
29. *Votive painting, the gift of Queen Mary Josephine (1753)*

The Treasury (1649–1653)

Silver cross of King Sigismund I (1510)

Monstrance, a gift from King Sigismund I (1542)

Hungarian cassock, from the late 15th century

The so-called Kordecki Monstrance, by the Warsaw goldsmith Venceslaus Grottke (1672)

Monstrance, a gift of Sztyftowski (1721)

Altar in ebony and silver – a gift of Prince Constantine Sobieski, a Habsburg work (1624)

*Meissen porcelain a gift of
Augustus III of Saxony (1744)*

Gilded silver chalice, a gift of
Francis Lubomirski (1743)

The reliquary of St. John Nepomucen, 17th c.

Monstrance and candelabra, offered
by the Austrian Imperial family (17th c.)

Gilded bronze clock, the gift of King John III
Sobieski, an Augsburg work (17th century).
Showing years, months, days and hours

8. THE LIBRARY

The Jasna Góra monastery has a celebrated library rich in volumes. The most valuable include ancient Polish and foreign prints (about 8.000), as well as unique examples and priceless manuscripts. They feature hand-painted illustrations some from the Jagellonian collection donated to the monastery.

Before the 1690 fire, part of the belltower was used as a library. The Pauline Monks built the new library in the west wing of the new monastery between 1736 and 1739.

The internal decoration of the library was the work of the monk, Gregory Woźniakowic, who made the tables and shelves with various wood inlaid with different tones. The volumes' containers are in wood, backed with leather and gold. This combination of gold and wood-brown makes for a warm, elegant atmosphere.

The library's ceiling adds to its beauty and is enriched with various frescoes, probably the work of an Italian artist. In the centre, a theological discussion is depicted and around it, are frescoes on the contemplative life and study. Since 1920 the library has had a representative function, hosting the meetings of the Polish Episcopal Conference.

Monastery ,the old Library

A fragment of the ancient book collection

*Library ,
Inlaid table*

9. THE KNIGHTS' HALL

Along the monastery's southern facade and beside the Chapel of the Virgin, the Knights' Hall is located. It was constructed in 1647 in Renaissance style and is characterised by the richness and harmony of its architecture. (Its cornices and the capitals of its columns are famous). The Knights' Hall has an eminently representative function for Jasna Góra. Nine 17th century paintings (the Jasna Góra school) adorn the walls and depict important events in the monastery's history. Various regimental flags from the World Wars are also featured. At the far end of the hall there is the altar of St. John the

The Knights' Hall

Evangelist, of the 18th century.

The Knights' Hall was the venue for the Diet's debates during the reign of John Casimir (1657) and in later years, it hosted meetings and official gatherings as well as the annual theological and philosophical conferences of ecclesiastical scholars. In 1936, the first plenary Synod of the Polish Church was held in this Hall.

Stairs leading to the Knights' Hall

10. THE REFECTORY

The refectory is situated in the monastery's west wing in the room below the library on the ground floor. It is a 17th century construction.

The refectory's ceiling is covered with elaborate, multi-coloured stucco work with a darker dominating tone and is probably by Karl Dankwart.

The marriage beween King Michael Korybut Wiśniowiecki and the Archuduchess Eleanor of Austria was celebrated here. In the vault's centre, a nuptial crown commemorates the event.

Monastery , Refectory (dinning room)

The entrance to the Chapel

The interior of the Chapel

11. THE SACRED CHAPEL OF THE POLISH NATION

The Sacred Chapel of the Polish Nation is situated in a 17th century building facing south west near the bastion and between the basilica and the monument to Fr Kordecki (the heroic defender o Jasna Góra in 1655). The Chape bears his name.

The Chapel, which was de dicated on May 3, 1989, conserves reliquaries of patriotic value: urns with the ashes of Polish soliders and earth soaked with the blood of sol diers who fought for Poland's inde pendence in various epochs. There are also a number of memoria tablets.

Some urns contain earth stained with the blood of soldier; who fought in the 1831 and 185; Insurrections, during World War I during the 1920 war against the Bolsheviks and during World War I (in action at Westerplatte, Monte Cassino, Tobrśk, Narvik, Arnhem Falaise and Kołobrzeg).

Also to be found are the ashes of soldiers who died in action during the Insurrection of Warsav (1944), of soldiers of the Nationa Army (A.K. the Armia Krajowa), and of troops and civilians massacred ir the various German and Russian extermination camps of Stalin.

Some urns contain earth soaked with the blood of the wor kers of Poznań, Radom, Gdańsk and Silesia and commemorate Poland' traumatic post-war history. Also con served in a special urn is earth from the site of Fr. George Popiełuszko' martyrdom.

2. THE 600ᵀᴴ ANNIVERSARY MUSEUM

In the rooms of the monastery's old printing house, which the Russians destroyed ruring the partition of Poland in 1864, a museum was opened documenting the icon's 600 years at Jasna Góra and the history of the Pauline Monks. A rich collection of paintings, mostly by the monks themselves, are testimonies of the Order's activities since it was founded in 1250.

The museum also houses a considerable collection of mainly liturgical objects of great artistic value, which the monks manufactured at Jasna Góra in the 17th and 18th centuries.

In the central glass case, three of the seven famous robes covering the image of the Virgin are on show. A special menton is due to documents on the sanctuary's foundation, two bearing the seal of prince Ladislaus of Opole and the date 1382 and one of King Vladislaus Jagiełło, dated 1393. The museum also features the votive offerings of the survivors of the Oświęcim (Auschwitz) and Dachau concentration camps, the Nobel Peace Prize Medal of Lech Wałęsa and various gifts of Pope John Paul II: an ivory statuette of the Virgin, a pastoral staff and two chalices. Of particular interest are the ancient musical instruments on display, especially the wind instruments used on special liturgical occasions and at the beginning and the end of the ostensorium of the Icon every day.

Interior of the Museum

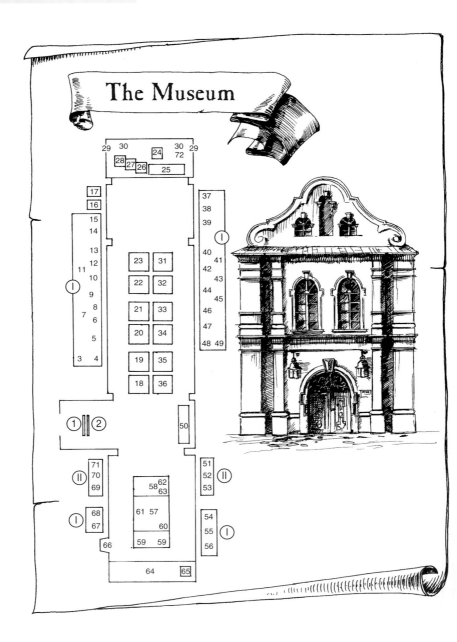

The Museum

THE MUSEUM

I. *Paintings of the Jasna Góra school (XVII century)*

II. *Panels from the ancient cases safeguarding the treasure (XVII century)*

1. *St. Paul the First Hermit and St. Anthony the Abbot*

2. *Pope John XXII confers the Regola of St. Augustine on the Paulines*

3. *St. Andrew Świerad (+ 1034 ca.)*

4. *St. Benedict, a hermit (+ 1037)*

5. *Jasper Biedrzychowski, the Paulines Provincial (+ 1630)*

6. *The Blessed Luke, a Hungarian Pauline (XV century)*

7. *The death of the Blessed Vladislaw Batory, a Pauline*

8. *The death of the Blessed Philip in the Hungarian Pauline monastery (XVI century)*

9. *Andrew Gołdonowski, the Pauline Provincial between 1641 and 1644*

10. *The Jagelloni family receive Holy Communion at Jasna Góra (1477)*

11. *Prince Vladislaw of Opole donates the painting of the Virgin to the Paulines (1382)*

12. *The Pauline Stanislaw Oporowski preaching (+ 1552)*

13. *Nicholas Staszewski, the Pauline Genera between 1640 and 1644*

14. *The Jasna Góra Jubilee (1882)*

15. *King Siegmund I offers the Paulines the reliquary of the Holy Cross*

16. *"Prayer for reconciliation" in a painting by L. Sobocki (1982)*

17. *"The Pastor of hope" in a painting by L. Sobocki (1981)*

18. *The reliquary of St. Paul the First Hermit (XVIII century)*

19. *The Pauline Code (1512) and the Rosary of Fr. Augustine Kordecki*

20. *The founding document of Jasna Góra of Prince Vladislaw of Opole (August, 2, 1382)*

21. *The founding document of Jasna Góra of King Wlasilaw Jagiełło (February 24, 1393)*

22. *Cross with a clock (XVII century); volumes from the monastery's printing house (XVIII century)*

23. *Field altar (XIX century); volumes from the monastery's printing house (XIX century)*

24. *A panel in cedar wood behind the Icon (XVII century)*

25. *The cope of the canonical vestments of Michael Krassowski (1745)*

26. *The Image's coral vestment (1910)*

27. *The vestment "of the Millenium" (1966)*

28. *The vestment "of the Sixth Centenary" (1982)*

29. *Funeral portraits and votive plates (XVII-XVIII centuries)*

30. *Votive plates (XVIII-XIX centuries); amber and coral necklaces*

31. *Votive badges and medals (XIX-XX centuries)*

32. *A votive offering of Lech Wałęsa*

33. *A votive offering for miracles of healing (XIX century)*

34. *A votive offering of deportees to Siberia, of concentration camp prisoners and of Solidarność members jailed during the state of war (1981)*

35. *Gifts of John Paul II*

36. *Chalices and Jubilee medals (XVII-XX centuries)*

37. *St. Luke painting the Icon of the Virgin*

38. *A self-portrait by Paulite Augustine Jędrzejczyk (1939)*

39. *Augustine Kordecki, the Prior of Jasna Góra (1655)*

40. *The Blessed Thomas, a Paulite (+ 1488)*

41. *Pope Urban IV gives his approval to the Order of St. Paul the First Hermit*

42. *The martyrdom of the Paulites in Hungary (1526)*

43. *Tobias Czechowicz, Paulites' Provincial (+ 1703) in a posthumous portrait*

Museum, Robes from the Miraculous Icon of Our Lady

The Pauline Code (1512)

*Museum, the reliquary of
St. Paul the First Hermit (1731)*

St. Paul the First Hermit

Museum, votive offerings of Polish Martyrs

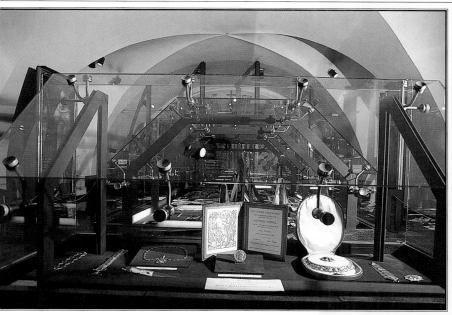

Museum, showcase with votive offerings

*Museum, the reliquary of St. Paul
the First Hermit (1731)*

13. THE MARIAN ROOM

The building is situated to the right of the sanctuary's main entrance and is used for temporary exhibitions. Once the lodgings of the sanctuary's maintenance workers, it was transformed into a room of penitence in 1920. In the 1950s, it hosted a Marian exhibition from which its present name derives. Since then, it has been used for various exhibitions on the life of the Chruch in Poland and on the activities of the Marian Sanctuary.

Also conserved in the Room are some mementos of the President of the Polish Republic, Ignatiu Mościcki and of Primate Stefan Wyszyński, Cardinal. Some items bear witness to the suffering of Poland during this century and there is also a collection of large votive candles from all over the world.

Marian Room

Marian Room, candles and other votive gifts

Marian Room, showcase with votive offerings

5th Pilgrimage The Holy Father to the Homeland

14. THE ROBES FOR THE HOLY PICTURE

The tradition of dressing the painting of the Virgin dates back to the time of its arrival at Jasna Góra. Originally, the precious items were nailed on to the painting. After the restoration of 1430, the painting's backdrop was covered in sheets of gold and silver inlaid with crowns. The current custom of adorning the Virgin and Child dates back to the second half of the 17th century.

Seven robes currently exist each with its own name. The most precious are of diamonds and

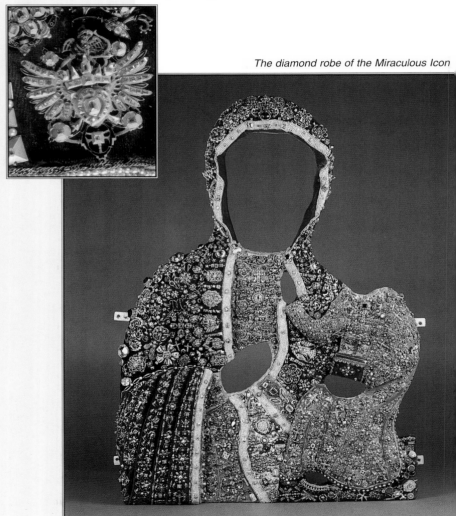

The diamond robe of the Miraculous Icon

rubies and constitute a collection of old gems from the 15th and 19th centuries. The two robes in coral are very beautiful.

A special robe was made for the occasion of Poland's baptism, the Millenium celebrations in 1966, and is encrusted with rubies and wedding rings giving it its name - "The Robe of Fidelity". Two robes were also made for the sanctuary's 600th Jubilee Year. The gems and other precious stones were fixed on rigid velvet cushions and today, the robes constitute rare examples of artistic work in gold.

The ruby robe of the Miraculous Image

The coral robe of the Miraculous Image

15. THE ARSENAL

A construction of the 17th century, the arsenal of the Jasna Góra fortress served its purpose until 1813. In 1969, it was transformed into a military museum.

It currently features three sections of different themes regarding military history, the history of the fortress and the votive offering of soldiers.

Among the most historically valuable exhibits are the cannonballs the Swedish invaders fired in their 1655 attack on the sancturary; the gifts of King John Sobieski III after the victory over the Turks at Vienna in 1683; the sabres and batons of the Polish Field Marshals; the votive offerings of Polish People deported to Siberia after the 1863 insurrection against the Russians and a rich collection of medals donated by solidiers and civilians in the 17th and 20th centuries.

The Arsenal

THE ARSENAL
I. Weapons and firearms
  (XVII-XX centuries)
II. The history of
  the Jasna Góra fortress
III. A votive offering made by solidiers

1. The official documents of
  the fortress (XIX-XX centuries)
2. Medals, crosses and military
  and civilian insignia
3. The Virgin, Patron of the Army
  adorned with medals nad crosses
  offered by soldiers (1977)
4. The silver crown over the image of
  the Virgin (XIX century)
5. Military standards (1919-1943)
6. The Swedish siege (1655). A copy of
  the 1659 lithograph by J. Bensheimer
7. The armoury typical of the defenders
  of Jasna Góra during the siege (1655)
8. The Swedish siege. A 1982 painting
  by F. Fellman, from the XVII century
  original
9. Augustine Kordecki, the Superior of
  Jasna Góra (1655). Painting by
  P. Cieślewski (1853)
10. The remains of Swedish bombs and
  grenades (1655)
11. A Turkish sword of the XVI century,
  a gift of King Stephen Batory
12. A Turkish sabre of the XVI century,
  a gift of Stanisław Żółkiewski
13. The bulava mace of Martin
  Kalinowski, a 1650 gift
14. The bulava mace of Stanisław
  Rewera Potocki, a 1655 gift
15. The bulava mace of Timothy
  Cieciura, the gift of King John
  Casimir in 1661
16. The bulava mace of Stanisław
  Jabłonowski, a 1684 gift
17. The bulava mace of Joseph
  Potocki (XVII century)
18. The bulava mace and sabre of
  Marshal Edward Rydz Śmigły (1936)
19. The coat of arms of King
  John III Sobieski
20. A Turkish helmet and chainmail
  (XVII century)
21. Oriental carpets (XVII century)
22. The drapes of the field mosque of the
  Grand Vizier Kara Mustafa (1683)
23. King John III Sobieski at Jasna Góra
  before the Battle of Vienna. A 1982

painting by F. Fellman, from the
XVII century oryginal
24. A Tartar bunciuk (the sign of power),
  the gift of James Sobieski in 1772
25. Turkish weapons (XVI-XVII centuries),
  the gift of King John III Sobieski
26. John III Sobieski in the Chapel of the
  Virgin before the Battle of Vienna.
  A painting by John Matejko of 1859
27. A fragment of the insignia of King
  John III Sobieski, a 1772 gift
28. Votive plaques in silver (XVII century)
29. The ruffs of the Bar Confederates
  (1768-1772)
30. The cross of the Bar Confederates
  (1771)
31. The Confederates, led by Casimir
  Pulaski, defend Jasna Góra. A 1982
  painting by A. Krupska, from
  J. Chełmoński's original of 1875
32. Stanisław Augustine Poniatowski
  (1780 ca.)
33. The drumstick of the principal drum
  of the Orchestra of the 17th Infantry
  Regiment, Grand Duchy of Warsaw
34. The defence of Jasna Góra against
  the Austrians (1809)
35. The white eagle, a sketch by John
  Matejko (XIX century)
36. A small cross of the Order of the
  Golden Fleece, the gift of King
  Vladislaw IV Waza (1633)
37. The White Eagle Medal, the gift of
  the voivoda of Sandomierz,
  John Tarło (1750)
38. Polish medals of the period of the
  Grand Duchy of Warsaw
  (18097-1814) and of the November
  Insurrection (1831)
39. Russian medals (XIX-XX centuries)
40. Decorations with patriotic symbols
  and designs (XIX-XX centuries)
41. Decorations with patriotic symbols
  and designs (XX century)
42. World War II decorations with
  patriotic symbols and designs
43. World War I and II name badges
  donated by soldiers
44. The votive offering of deportees to
  Siberia (1864) and of World War II
  solidiers and prisoners

The Arsenal

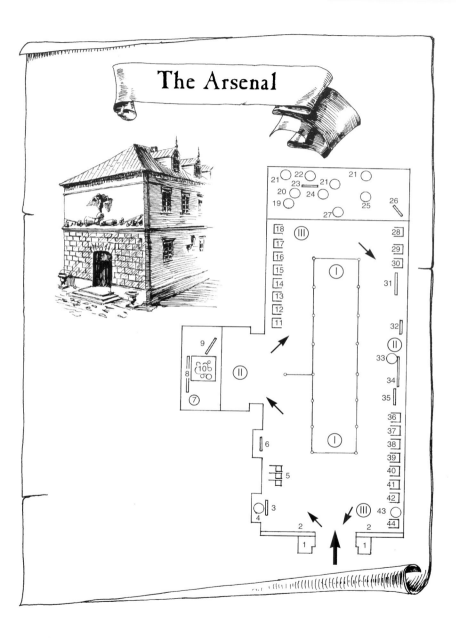

Halberds, the Arsenal

Arsenal, a Turkish sabre

*Arsenal, the Patroness of the army, the
Virgin Mary, replica of the miraculous
Icon, adorned with medals and crosses
of honour offered by soldiers*

Arsenal Exhibition of items commemorating the glorious defence against the Swedes in 1655

Arsenal, Central wall. The gifts of King John Sobieski after the 1683 victory at Vienna

Arsenal. Painting of John III Sobieski in the Chapel of the Virgin before the 1683 victory of Vienna

6. THE STATIONS OF THE CROSS

In 1913 in the park around the sanctuary, once the fortress' moat, the 14 Stations of the Cross have been erected to designs by Stefan Szyller. The figures of the 14 stations, in bronze, are by the sculptor Pius Weloński. It is part of Jasna Góra's tradition that nearly every group of pilgrims celebrates the Stations of the Cross.

Some pass from one station to another on their knees. These permanent stations along the walls are a demonstration that Christ is the core of this Marian sanctuary.

*The Stations of the Cross
in Jasna Góra*

17. THE PILGRIMS

Jasna Góra's pilgrim tradition was born with the sancturary. In a short time, it became Poland's most famous sanctuary because of the grace and miracles received from the Virgin.

In 1429, the Polish King Ladislaus Jagiełło told Pope Martin V in a letter that the sanctuary was self-supporting thanks to the offerings of the numerous pilgrims who visited Jasna Góra in faith and hope. The icon's profanation in 1430 and the solemn procession following its restoration attracted even more pilgrims. In 1582, Pope Gregory XIII's representative, Antonio Pescevino, met with the Polish King Stephen Batory and marvelled at the vast numbers of pilgrims. He said Jasna Góra was "Poland's Loreto".

In the 17th century, an average of 100,000 pilgrims a year were visiting the sancturary. They included kings, cossacks, aristocrats and dignitaries as well as the ordinary faithful. Later, it became the custom

to make pilgrimages on foot and the tradition has remained unchanged for centuries in some Polish cities: Żywiec since 1611, Gliwice since 1627, Kraków since 1683 and Kalisz since the first half of the 17th century. (The faithful of this city also return to their homes on foot.) The most imposing pilgrimage, from Warsaw, is the prototype and was begun in 1711 under the guidance of the Pauline Monks. The history of this pilgrimage has known drama: in 1792, cossacks attacked and massacred all the pilgrims.

During the period of the partition of Poland (1772-1819), numerous pilgrims continued to gather at Jasna Góra despite the difficulties, the prohibitions and the unjust politics of the time.

During the sanctuary's fifth centenary year (1882), about 400,000 faithful visited Jasna Góra.

At the beginning of this century, Jasna Góra was attracting up to one million pilgrims a year so a project was devised to organise pilgrimages according to social groups. The project envisaged organising the pilgrimages according to evangelical ideals. The project was realised and became established after 1945 and today, it constitutes one of the unusual characteristics of Polish pilgrimages.

Immediately after the War, about one million faithful were still visiting the sanctuary. But in 1951, the Communist regime devised a project to cover all the pathways leading to Jasna Góra with grass which meant the suspension of pilgrimages on foot except for the pilgrimage from Warsaw. Despite these difficulties, one million pilgrims managed to visit the sanctuary on the occasion of the "Vows of the Nation" pronounced on August 26, 1956. In the years to come, which would feature the "Great Novena" in preparation for Poland's Millenium celebrations in 1966, and in the light of the Second Vatican Council, pilgrimages increased once more.

Cardinal Wyszyński helped greatly in this for he summoned all the faithful to kneel before the Virgin of Jasna Góra. The Sanctuary has given the Polish people the strength to survive and confirm the country's Christianity. In 1970, pilgrims were numbering as many as two million. This number was to grow considerably on the election to the Chair of Peter of Cardinal Wojtyła.

Between June 4 and 6, 1979 about three and a half million pilgrims gathered at Jasna Góra and many of them had arrived there on foot, to see Pope John Paul II. The workers launched the idea of organised pilgrimages (and left their mark on them in a sense), by gathering at Jasna Góra in 1981 during what was called the "peaceful revolution" from whose fruits Poland and the rest of Europe are benefitting.

Between 1981 and 1990 about 300,000 people have participated in pilgrimages every year for a total of four million. The pilgrimages are organised according to all the social brackets: workers and farmers, students and teachers, intellectuals and railway workers, doctors and lawyers, soldiers and policemen, politicians and State representatives as well as bishops and ecclesiastical authorities.

The participation of pilgrims from Europe and from al

over the world is significant because of the spiritual dimension of pilgrimages to Jasna Góra.

In 1989 2353 groups from 91 countries visited the sanctuary. Foreigners have been taking part in pilgrimages on foot since 1966 and several thousand have visited Jasna Góra in recent years.

Pilgrimages on foot are a distinctive feature of Polish Catholicism today. They usually last several days so they provide an opportunity for evangelisation which bears witness to a spiritual retreat on the move, to rediscover our capicity to love our neighbours.

Pilgrimages on foot to Jasna Góra, in which representatives of various European countries participate, can play an important role in building Europe's "common home", in forming a community of nations in a new Europe, able to live in real solidarity and fraternity.

*Pope John Paul II,
a pilgrim to Jasna Gora*

18. THE JASNA GÓRA APPEAL - EVENING PRAYERS

Every evening at nine o'clock, the bells of the Jasna Góra sanctuary invite the faithful to prayer as part of the special Jasna Góra Appeal, dear to the heart of every Polish man and woman. At this hour, the faithful to the Mother of God in Poland and throughout the world gather in spirit before the miraculous painting of Jasna Góra. They are invited to pray every single evening at the end of the day, giving voice to the Jasna Góra pilgrim, giving voice to man, the pilgrim of the earth.

The origins of the Jasna Góra Appeal date back to the imprisonment of Primate Stefan Wyszyński under the Stalinist regime. On December 8, 1954, the appeal for the Church, for Poland and for the Primate's freedom was first read in the Chapel of the Miraculous Painting.

The Appeal begins with the singing of the oldest Polish Marian hymn, the "Bogurodzica" which was Poland's national anthem for many years. During the hymn, the silver screen which covers the miraculous Image of the Mother of God is raised and all sing the Appeal three times: "Mary, Queen of Poland, I stand before You, I remember I am watching !" After this, the priest leads the faithful in a short Marian meditation and then raises prayers for the Church, for the world and for all men to the Mother of God.

A mystery of the Rosary is recited for intentions and a special prayer for the Pope, the Vicar of Christ, follows. There is then a final benediction. The Appeal prayers end with a Marian hymn during which the Image is covered.

International Youth Meeting (August 1991)

*Pope John Paul II 5th Pilgrimage to Poland. Archbishop of Czestochowa Stanislaw Nowak,
Bishop Antoni Długosz and Father John Pach of the Jasna Gora Monastery*

Papal Blessing of one million faithful

19. USEFUL INFORMATION ABOUT THE SANCTUARY

JASNA GÓRA - SANKTUARY OF THE POLISH NATION
42-225 Częstochowa, ul. O. A. Kordeckiego 2
tel. 0048/(0)34/65 66 88; fax 0048/(0)34/65 67 28
Account No: PKO II/O Częstochowa 10201664-117740-270-1

Jasna Góra is open from 5^{00} a.m. until 9^{30} p.m.

5^{30} a.m.- Hymn to Our Lady;
6^{00} a.m.- The screen covering the Miracolous Paiting of Our Lady is raised;
      Holy Masses in The Chapel of Our Lady are at the times:
      6^{00}, 7^{00}, 7^{30}, 8^{00}, 9^{30}, 11^{00} a.m. and 3^{30}, 6^{30} p.m.;
      With an Additional Saturday Mass at 12^{00};
      Sundays and Holydays at 12^{00} and 8^{30} p.m.;
      At 8^{45} a.m. and 5^{45} p.m. It is possible to attend Holy Mass in a Foreign
Language;
10^{00} a.m. - 3^{30} p.m. - Adoration of The Blessed Sacrament in the Sacred Heart Chapel;
      /The Basilica - Tuesdays to Fridays/;
12^{00} - The screen covering the Miracolous Paiting of Our Lady is lowered;
      /on Saturdays, Sundays and Holydays at 13^{00} p.m./*;
1^{30} p.m. - The screen covering the Miracolous Paiting of Our Lady is raised;
      /on working days during the months of May through to September/*;
2^{00} p.m.- The screen covering the Miracolous Paiting of Our Lady is raised;
      /on Saturdays and Holydays during the months of May through to September/*
3^{00} p.m.- The screen covering the Miracolous Paiting of Our Lady is raised;
      /after the pilgrim season/*;
4^{00} p.m.- Holy Rosary;
6^{00} p.m.- Novena /only Saturdays/;
9^{00} p.m.- The Jasna Góra Appeal - Evening Prayers;
9^{30} p.m.- 4^{30} a.m. - Night prayers and meditations /only if organised previously/.

It is possible to have The Sacrament of Reconcilation in many languages - only at the
Sacristy - also can be arranget at the Jasna Góra Centre of Information.

---

* These times can vary aspecially when there are so many pilgrims within the Sanctuary.